The Peach Cookbook

Laura Sommers is **The Recipe Lady!**

She is the #1 Best Selling Author of over 80 recipe books.

She is a loving wife and mother who lives on a small farm in Baltimore County, Maryland and has a passion for all things domestic especially when it comes to saving money. She has a profitable eBay business and is a couponing addict. Follow her tips and tricks to learn how to make delicious meals on a budget, save money or to learn the latest life hack!

Visit her Amazon Author Page to see her latest books:

amazon.com/author/laurasommers

Visit the Recipe Lady's blog for even more great recipes and to learn which books are **FREE** for download each week:

http://the-recipe-lady.blogspot.com/

Subscribe to The Recipe Lady blog through Amazon and have recipes and updates sent directly to your Kindle:

The Recipe Lady Blog through Amazon

Laura Sommers is also an Extreme Couponer and Penny Hauler! If you would like to find out how to get things for **FREE** with coupons or how to get things for only a **PENNY**, then visit her couponing blog **Penny Items and Freebies**

http://penny-items-and-freebies.blogspot.com/

© Copyright 2017. Laura Sommers.
All rights reserved.
No part of this book may be reproduced in any form or by any electronic or mechanical means without written permission of the author. All text, illustrations and design are the exclusive property of
Laura Sommers

Introduction	1
Peach Cobbler	2
Peach Pie	3
Peach Avocado Salsa	4
Spicy Peach Chutney	5
Mango, Peach and Pineapple Salsa	6
Peach Crisp	7
Peach Avocado Salsa	8
Peach Preserves	9
Spiced Habanero Peach Jam	10
Peach Gelee Candy	12
Ginger-Peach Jam	13
Peach Upside Down Cake	14
Sweet Georgia Peach and Pecan Dip	15
Pickled Peaches	16
Baked Pancake with Peaches	17
Raspberry-Peach Pie	18
Peach Pound Cake	19
Peach Curd	20
Peach Financiers	21
Spiced Blackberry and Peach Compote	22
Peach and Blackberry Cobbler	23
Peach Muffins	24
Spiced Peach Oatmeal Muffins	25
Peach, Basil & Cheddar Muffins	26

Peach Sweet and Sour Sauce	27
Tuna Fish Tacos	28
Peach Sangria	29
Honeyed Peach Pancake Syrup	30
Mascarpone Stuffed French Toast with Peaches	31
Champagne Peach Punch	32
Peach Apple Salsa	33
Peach Pear Salsa	34
Spicy Strawberry Kiwi Peach Salsa	35
Peach and Strawberry Sorbet	36
Peach and Lavender Ice	37
Georgia Peach Homemade Ice Cream	38
Peach Pie with Sour Cream	39
Grilled Peaches and Cream	40
Peaches and Cream	41
Grilled Peaches	42
Peach Brulee	43
Peach Bread Pudding with Caramel Sauce	44
Peaches and Cream Pie	45
Peach and Escarole Salad	46
Peach and Berry Salad	47
Peach Salad with Raspberry Vinaigrette	48
Minty Peach Chicken Salad	49
Peach and Tomato Caprese Salad	50
Peach Bow Tie Salad	51
Peach Smoothie	52
Peach Banana Smoothie	53

Peach Pudding	54
About the Author	55
Other books by Laura Sommers	56

Introduction

Peaches are a wholesome fruit that is both delicious and versatile. Sweet succulent peaches are America's favorite fruit. This cookbook contains many recipes with the peach as the starring role. There are deserts, breads, muffins, pies and cobblers.

There are a variety of recipes for beverages, marinades and appetizers. If you enjoy peaches, you will love this cookbook and its many ways to prepare your favorite fruit.

Peach Cobbler

Ingredients:

1 cup all-purpose flour
1/2 cup brown sugar
1/2 cup white sugar
2 tsps. baking powder
1/2 tsp. salt
1 tsp. vanilla extract
3/4 cup milk
1/2 cup margarine, melted
1 (29 oz.) can sliced canned peaches, drained
1 tsp. ground cinnamon

Directions:

1. Preheat oven to 400 degrees F (200 degrees C).
2. Grease a 9x9-inch baking dish.
3. In a large bowl, combine flour, brown sugar, white sugar, baking powder, salt, and vanilla.
4. Pour milk into dry ingredients, and then stir in melted margarine.
5. Mix thoroughly.
6. Pour mixture into prepared baking pan.
7. Arrange peaches on top and sprinkle with cinnamon.
8. Bake in preheated oven until golden brown, about 30 minutes.

Peach Pie

Ingredients:

1 (15 oz.) package pastry for a 9 inch double crust pie
1 egg, beaten 5 cups sliced peeled peaches
2 tbsps. lemon juice
1/2 cup all-purpose flour
1 cup white sugar
1/2 tsp. ground cinnamon
1/4 tsp. ground nutmeg
1/4 tsp. salt
2 tbsps. butter

Directions:

1. Preheat the oven to 450 degrees F (220 degrees C).
2. Line the bottom and sides of a 9 inch pie plate with one of the pie crusts. Brush with some of the beaten egg to keep the dough from becoming soggy later.
3. Place the sliced peaches in a large bowl, and sprinkle with lemon juice. Mix gently. In a separate bowl, mix together the flour, sugar, cinnamon, nutmeg and salt. Pour over the peaches, and mix gently.
4. Pour into the pie crust, and dot with butter.
5. Cover with the other pie crust, and fold the edges under. Flute the edges to seal or press the edges with the tines of a fork dipped in egg. Brush the remaining egg over the top crust.
6. Cut several slits in the top crust to vent steam.
7. Bake for 10 minutes in the preheated oven.
8. Reduce the heat to 350 degrees F (175 degrees C) and bake for an additional 30 to 35 minutes, until the crust is brown and the juice begins to bubble through the vents.
9. If the edges brown to fast, cover them with strips of aluminum foil about halfway through baking.
10. Cool before serving.

Peach Avocado Salsa

Ingredients:

2 fresh peaches - peeled, pitted, and diced
1 jalapeno pepper, seeded and minced
1/2 red onion, minced
1/2 red bell pepper, minced
1/4 cup chopped fresh cilantro, or to taste
2 cloves garlic, grated
1/2 lime, juiced
1/2 lemon, juiced
Salt and ground black pepper to taste
1 avocado, peeled, pitted, and diced

Directions:

1. Gently mix peaches, jalapeno pepper, red onion, red bell pepper, cilantro, garlic, lime juice, and lemon juice in a bowl; season with salt and black pepper.
2. Cover bowl with plastic wrap and refrigerate at least 30 minutes.
3. Fold avocado into the salsa to serve.

Spicy Peach Chutney

Ingredients:

4 lbs. sliced peeled peaches
1 cup raisins
2 cloves garlic, minced
1/2 cup chopped onion
5 oz. chopped preserved ginger
1 1/2 tbsps. chili powder
1 tbsp. mustard seed
1 tsp. curry powder
4 cups packed brown sugar
4 cups apple cider vinegar
1/4 cup pickling spice

Directions:

1. In a large heavy pot, stir together the peaches, raisins, garlic, onion, preserved ginger, chili powder, mustard seed, curry powder, brown sugar and cider vinegar.
2. Wrap the pickling spice in a cheesecloth bag, and place in the pot.
3. Bring to a boil, and cook over medium heat uncovered until the mixture reaches your desired consistency.
4. It will take about 1 1/2 hours to get a good thick sauce.
5. Stir frequently to prevent scorching on the bottom.
6. Remove the spice bag, and ladle into hot sterilized jars.
7. Wipe the rims with a clean moist cloth.
8. Seal with lids and rings, and process in a barely simmering water bath for 10 minutes, or the time recommended by your local extension for your area.
9. The water should cover the jars completely.

Mango, Peach and Pineapple Salsa

Ingredients:

2 mangos, peeled, seeded and chopped
2 small peaches, halved, pitted, and cut into 1/2-inch dice
1 cup diced fresh pineapple
4 tomatoes, chopped
1 white onion, diced
1 red bell pepper, diced
1 yellow bell pepper, diced
1 cup chopped fresh cilantro, or to taste
1 clove garlic, minced
1 small jalapeno pepper, minced
2 tbsps. lime juice
1 tsp. salt
2 tbsps. white sugar, or to taste
3/4 cup water

Directions:

1. Place the mango, peach, pineapple, tomato, onion, red pepper, yellow pepper, and cilantro in a mixing bowl.
2. Stir in the garlic, jalapeno, lime juice, salt, sugar, and water.
3. Cover and refrigerate at least 1 hour before serving.

Peach Crisp

Ingredients:

4 cups sliced fresh peaches
1/2 cup all-purpose flour
1/2 cup brown sugar
1/2 cup cold butter
1 tsp. ground cinnamon
1/4 tsp. salt
1 cup rolled oats

Directions:

1. Preheat oven to 350 degrees F (175 degrees C).
2. Arrange peaches evenly in an 8x8-inch baking dish.
3. Mix flour, brown sugar, butter, cinnamon, and salt in a bowl using a pastry cutter until evenly crumbled.
4. Fold oats into flour mixture; sprinkle and press topping into peaches.
5. Bake in the preheated oven until topping is lightly browned, about 30 minutes.

Peach Avocado Salsa

Ingredients:

2 fresh peaches, peeled, pitted, and diced
1 jalapeno pepper, seeded and minced
1/2 red onion, minced
1/2 red bell pepper, minced
1/4 cup chopped fresh cilantro, or to taste
2 cloves garlic, grated
1/2 lime, juiced
1/2 lemon, juiced
salt and ground black pepper to taste
1 avocado, peeled, pitted, and diced

Directions:

1. Gently mix peaches, jalapeno pepper, red onion, red bell pepper, cilantro, garlic, lime juice, and lemon juice in a bowl.
2. Season with salt and black pepper.
3. Cover bowl with plastic wrap and refrigerate at least 30 minutes.
4. Fold avocado into the salsa to serve.

Peach Preserves

Ingredients:

12 fresh peaches, pitted and chopped
4 1/2 cups white sugar
1 (2 oz.) pkg. dry pectin

Directions:

1. Crush 1 cup chopped peaches in the bottom of a large saucepan.
2. Add remaining peaches, and set pan over medium-low heat.
3. Bring to a low boil, and cook for about 20 minutes or until peaches become liquid (my family likes a few bits of peach left).
4. Pour peaches into a bowl, and then measure 6 cups back into the pan.
5. Add sugar, and bring to a boil over medium heat.
6. Gradually stir in dry pectin, and boil for 1 minute.
7. Remove from heat after 1 minute, and transfer to sterilized jars.
8. Process in hot water bath canner for 10 minutes. Let cool, and place on shelf.

Spiced Habanero Peach Jam

Ingredients:

3 1/2 pounds fresh peaches, peeled, pitted, and chopped
6 tbsps. lemon juice
1 vanilla bean, halved lengthwise and seeds scraped out
1 tsp. ground cinnamon
1 tsp. ground allspice
1/2 tsp. ground nutmeg
1/2 tsp. ground cardamom
2 habanero peppers, stemmed and seeded
2 (3 oz.) pouches liquid pectin
5 cups white sugar
2 cups packed brown sugar

Directions:

1. Put peaches in a Dutch oven or soup pot; stir in lemon juice, vanilla bean, cinnamon, allspice, nutmeg, and cardamom.
2. Place habanero peppers in a blender; top peppers with peach mixture.
3. Blend until mostly smooth; transfer mixture back to the Dutch oven.
4. Stir pectin into peach-habanero pepper mixture; bring to a full rolling boil.
5. Quickly stir white sugar and brown sugar into mixture; return to a boil, stirring constantly, until sugar is dissolved, about 2 minutes.
6. Sterilize the jars and lids in boiling water for at least 5 minutes.
7. Pack jam into the hot, sterilized jars, filling the jars to within 1/4 inch of the top.
8. Run a knife or a thin spatula around the insides of the jars after they have been filled to remove any air bubbles.
9. Wipe the rims of the jars with a moist paper towel to remove any food residue.
10. Top with lids, and screw on rings.
11. Place a rack in the bottom of a large stockpot and fill halfway with water. Bring to a boil and lower jars into the boiling water using a holder.
12. Leave a 2-inch space between the jars.
13. Pour in more boiling water if necessary to bring the water level to at least 1 inch above the tops of the jars.
14. Bring the water to a rolling boil, cover the pot, and process for 15 minutes.
15. Remove the jars from the stockpot and place onto a cloth-covered or wood surface, several inches apart, until cool.

16. Once cool, press the top of each lid with a finger, ensuring that the seal is tight (lid does not move up or down at all).
17. Store in a cool, dark area, and wait 1 to 2 weeks before opening for best results.

Peach Gelee Candy

Ingredients:

1 pound ripe peaches, peeled, pitted and sliced
1 tbsp. lime juice
2 cups white sugar, divided
3 tbsps. liquid pectin
1/2 cup white sugar, for sprinkling

Directions:

1. Line an 8x8-inch baking dish with plastic wrap.
2. Combine peaches and lime juice in a blender.
3. Puree until very smooth.
4. Pour into a saucepan over medium heat, stir in 1/2 cup sugar, and bring to a boil.
5. Cook, stirring continuously, until thickened, about 15 minutes.
6. Stir in remaining 1 1/2 cups sugar and pectin.
7. Using a thermometer, heat to 205 degrees F (96 degrees C) and cook, stirring continuously, for another 10 minutes.
8. Remove from heat.
9. Pour peach puree into the prepared baking dish.
10. Shake gently and tap on the countertop to remove any air bubbles. Cover and refrigerate at least 8 hours or overnight.
11. Sprinkle about half the 1/2 cup of sugar over a silicone baking mat and invert the peach gelee on top. Remove plastic wrap and sprinkle top with sugar.
12. Trim off any uneven edges and cut gelee into 25 squares.

Ginger-Peach Jam

Ingredients:

4 1/2 cups fresh peaches, peeled, pitted and chopped
1/4 cup finely chopped crystallized ginger
1 (1.75 oz.) pkg. powdered fruit pectin
6 cups white sugar
1/2 tsp. butter

Directions:

1. Bring peaches, ginger, and pectin to a boil in a large saucepan over medium heat. Stir in the sugar and butter; cook and stir until the sugar is dissolved. Return to a boil, stirring constantly for 1 minute more. Remove from heat, and skim off any foam with a spoon.
2. Sterilize the jars and lids in boiling water for at least 5 minutes.
3. Pack the peach jam into the hot, sterilized jars, filling the jars to within 1/4 inch of the top.
4. Run a knife or a thin spatula around the insides of the jars after they have been filled to remove any air bubbles.
5. Wipe the rims of the jars with a moist paper towel to remove any food residue.
6. Top with lids, and screw on rings.
7. Place a rack in the bottom of a large stockpot and fill halfway with water. Bring to a boil over high heat, then carefully lower the jars into the pot using a holder. Leave a 2 inch space between the jars.
8. Pour in more boiling water if necessary until the water level is at least 1 inch above the tops of the jars. Bring the water to a full boil, cover the pot, and process for 10 minutes.
9. Remove the jars from the stockpot and place onto a cloth-covered or wood surface, several inches apart, until cool.
10. Once cool, press the top of each lid with a finger, ensuring that the seal is tight (lid does not move up or down at all). Store in a cool, dark area.

Peach Upside Down Cake

Ingredients:

3 (15 oz.) cans sliced peaches in heavy syrup, drained well
5 tbsps. butter, melted
2/3 cup packed light brown sugar
1 tsp. cinnamon
1/2 tsp. nutmeg
1 1/2 sticks butter, softened
1 cup white sugar
2 large eggs
1/2 tsp. pure almond extract
2 cups flour
2 tsps. baking powder
1/2 tsp. salt
1 cup whole milk

Directions:

1. Spread peach slices between several layers of paper towels and let dry, gently pressing occasionally and replacing any soaked towels, 20 minutes.
2. Meanwhile, pour melted butter over bottom of a 6-quart oval slow cooker. Stir together brown sugar, cinnamon, and nutmeg in a bowl and sprinkle over butter.
3. Arrange peaches in a tight layer over brown sugar.
4. A partial second layer may be necessary to fit them all in.
5. Beat softened butter with white sugar in a large bowl with an electric mixer until light and fluffy, about 3 minutes.
6. Beat in eggs, 1 at a time, beating well after each addition.
7. Beat in almond extract.
8. Whisk together flour, baking powder, and salt in a separate bowl.
9. Working in batches, stir flour mixture into egg mixture alternately with milk, beginning and ending with flour mixture.
10. Mix batter until well combined. Spoon over peaches and spread evenly.
11. Drape paper towels over top of slow cooker (to absorb any condensation during baking), then cover with lid.
12. Cook on High until a wooden skewer inserted into center of cake comes out clean, 2 to 2 1/2 hours.
13. Remove lid and paper towels. Using oven mitts, remove ceramic liner from slow cooker and let cool 10 minutes.
14. Run a knife around edge of cake and carefully turn out onto a serving

Sweet Georgia Peach and Pecan Dip

Ingredients:

1 tbsp. butter
1/2 cup thinly sliced Vidalia onion 2 slices bacon, chopped
1 (1.25 oz.) pkg. brown sugar bourbon marinade mix
1 cup cola-flavored carbonated beverage
1/4 cup packed brown sugar
2 cups coarsely chopped fresh peaches
1/2 cup chopped pecans
2 (8 oz.) packages cream cheese, softened

Directions:

1. Melt butter in large skillet on medium-high heat. Add onion and bacon; cook and stir 6 to 8 minutes or until bacon is crisp.
2. Stir marinade mix, cola and brown sugar into skillet.
3. Bring just to boil.
4. Reduce heat to low; simmer 15 minutes or until mixture thickens slightly, stirring occasionally.
5. Stir in peaches and pecans; simmer until heated through.
6. Spread cream cheese evenly in bottom of 9-inch pie plate.
7. Top with warm peach mixture. Serve with assorted crackers or sliced French bread.

Pickled Peaches

Ingredients:

1 (15 oz.) can peach halves, undrained
1/4 cup white sugar
2 tbsps. vinegar
1/2 tsp. allspice
1/2 tsp. ground cloves

Directions:

1. Combine juice from canned peaches, sugar, vinegar, allspice, and cloves in a saucepan; bring to a boil.
2. Remove from heat and stir in peach halves. Let cool, about 15 minutes.
3. Cover saucepan with plastic wrap and refrigerate until flavors combine, 8 hours to overnight.

Baked Pancake with Peaches

Ingredients:

1 tbsp. butter
2 large peaches, peeled and cut into 1/4-inch slices
1 tbsp. brown sugar
1 tsp. ground cinnamon
3 eggs
1/2 cup milk
1/2 cup all-purpose flour
1 drop vanilla extract
1 pinch salt
1 pinch ground nutmeg

Directions:

1. Preheat oven to 425 degrees F (220 degrees C).
2. Melt butter in a cast-iron skillet in the preheating oven.
3. Combine peach slices, brown sugar, and cinnamon in a bowl.
4. Gently toss to coat the peaches well.
5. Beat eggs, milk, flour, vanilla extract, salt, and nutmeg together in a bowl until batter well-combined but a little lumpy; pour into skillet.
6. Top batter with the peach mixture.
7. Bake in preheated oven until set in the middle, about 20 minutes.

Raspberry-Peach Pie

Ingredients:

1 (10 oz.) package frozen unsweetened raspberries, thawed
1 (10 oz.) package frozen unsweetened sliced peaches
1 1/3 cups white sugar, divided
6 tbsps. all-purpose flour
1 prepared double pie crust

Directions:

1. Preheat an oven to 450 degrees F (230 degrees C).
2. Mix raspberries, peaches, 1 cup sugar, and flour in a large bowl.
3. Press one pie crust into a pie dish.
4. Pour fruit mixture into pie crust.
5. Sprinkle remaining 1/3 cup sugar over fruit.
6. Cut designs in the second pie crust using a cookie cutter and arrange pie crust over fruit.
7. Pinch the edges of the bottom and top crusts together to seal.
8. Bake in the preheated oven for 10 minutes.
9. Reduce oven temperature to 375 degrees F (190 degrees C) and continue baking until crust is golden brown and fruit filling is bubbly, about 35 minutes more.

Peach Pound Cake

Ingredients:

1 cup butter or margarine, softened
2 cups white sugar
4 eggs
1 tsp. vanilla extract
3 cups all-purpose flour
1 tsp. baking powder
1/2 tsp. salt
2 cups fresh peaches, pitted and chopped

Directions:

1. Preheat oven to 325 degrees F (165 degrees C).
2. Butter a 10 inch tube pan and coat with white sugar.
3. In a large bowl, cream together the butter and sugar until light and fluffy.
4. Add the eggs one at a time, beating well with each addition, then stir in the vanilla.
5. Reserve 1/4 cup of flour for later, and sift together the remaining flour, baking powder and salt.
6. Gradually stir into the creamed mixture.
7. Use the reserved flour to coat the chopped peaches, then fold the floured peaches into the batter.
8. Spread evenly into the prepared pan.
9. Bake for 60 to 70 minutes in the preheated oven, or until a toothpick inserted into the cake comes out clean.
10. Allow cake to cool in the pan for 10 minutes, before inverting onto a wire rack to cool completely.

Peach Curd

Great on scones, toast or pound cake.

Ingredients:

3 fresh peaches, halved and pitted
4 cups white sugar
2 eggs
4 egg yolks
1 tbsp. lemon juice
1 tsp. rose water (optional)
3/4 cup butter

Directions:

1. Blend peach halves in a blender until smooth; transfer to a large bowl.
2. Beat sugar, eggs, egg yolks, lemon juice, and rose water into peach puree until incorporated.
3. Melt butter in the top of a double boiler over simmering water.
4. Stir peach mixture into melted butter, stirring constantly, until curd is thickened, 5 to 10 minutes.
5. Sterilize jars and lids in boiling water for at least 5 minutes.
6. Pack peach curd into the hot, sterilized jars, filling the jars to within 1/4 inch of the top. Run a knife or a thin spatula around the insides of the jars after they have been filled to remove any air bubbles.
7. Wipe the rims of the jars with a moist paper towel to remove any food residue.
8. Top with lids, and screw on rings.
9. Place a rack in the bottom of a large stockpot and fill halfway with water. Bring to a boil and lower jars into the boiling water using a holder.
10. Leave a 2-inch space between the jars.
11. Pour in more boiling water if necessary to bring the water level to at least 1 inch above the tops of the jars.
12. Bring the water to a rolling boil, cover the pot, and process for 10 minutes.
13. Remove the jars from the stockpot and place onto a cloth-covered or wood surface, several inches apart, until cool.
14. Once cool, press the top of each lid with a finger, ensuring that the seal is tight (lid does not move up or down at all).
15. Store in a cool dark area.

Peach Financiers

Ingredients:

3 oz. unsalted butter plus additional for greasing
3 egg whites
1/2 cup white sugar
1/2 cup almond meal
3 tbsps. all-purpose flour plus additional for dusting pan
1/4 tsp. vanilla extract
1/8 tsp. salt
12 small pieces of peeled peach

Directions:

1. Preheat oven to 400 degrees F.
2. Generously butter a 12-muffin mini-muffin tin. Add a pinch of flour to each cup; shake to coat bottoms.
3. Melt butter in a saucepan over medium heat.
4. The melted butter will get foamy. Keep pan moving to prevent burning, but continue toasting butter until it turns golden brown, about 4 minutes.
5. Remove from heat.
6. Whisk egg whites and sugar together in a large bowl.
7. Whisk until sugar dissolves and egg whites get thick and foamy, 2 or 3 minutes.
8. Mix in almond meal, flour, vanilla, and salt.
9. Whisk in browned butter.
10. Fill muffin cups almost to the cop.
11. Tap pan to eliminate any air bubbles.
12. Bake 5 minutes. Remove pan from oven, and top financiers with small pieces of peach. Transfer pan back to oven.
13. Continue baking until browned, 10 to 12 more minutes.
14. Let cool at least 10 minutes before removing from the pan.

Spiced Blackberry and Peach Compote

Ingredients:

3 tbsps. butter
2 tbsps. maple sugar
2 tsps. grated fresh ginger
1 tsp. ground cinnamon
1/2 tsp. freshly grated nutmeg
3 cups frozen peach slices
1 cup frozen blackberries

Directions:

1. Melt butter in a saucepan over medium heat.
2. Stir maple sugar, ginger, cinnamon, and nutmeg into the melted butter.
3. Add peaches and stir to coat.
4. Cook the peaches at a simmer until soft and the juices begin to thicken, about 20 minutes.
5. Gently fold blackberries into the peach mixture.
6. Cook until the berries soften, about 5 minutes more.

Peach and Blackberry Cobbler

Ingredients:

4 cups peeled and sliced fresh peaches
1 cup fresh blackberries
1/4 cup white sugar
1 tsp. ground cinnamon
1 tbsp. lemon juice
1/2 cup butter, melted
1 1/4 cups all-purpose flour
1 cup white sugar
2 tsps. baking powder
1/2 tsp. salt
1 cup milk

Directions:

1. Preheat oven to 350 degrees F (175 degrees C).
2. Mix peaches, blackberries, 1/4 cup sugar, cinnamon, and lemon juice in a bowl.
3. Pour butter into a 9x13-inch glass baking dish and evenly coat the bottom and sides.
4. Whisk flour, 1 cup sugar, baking powder, and salt in a bowl.
5. Mix in milk, stirring just to moisten dry ingredients.
6. Pour batter into prepared baking dish and distribute fruit mixture evenly over the batter.
7. Bake in the preheated oven until cobbler is golden brown, about 45 minutes.

Peach Muffins

Ingredients:

3 cups all-purpose flour
1 tbsp. ground cinnamon
1 tsp. baking soda
1 tsp. salt
1 1/4 cups vegetable oil
3 eggs, lightly beaten
2 cups white sugar
2 cups peeled, pitted, and chopped peaches

Directions:

1. Preheat oven to 400 degrees F (200 degrees C).
2. Lightly grease 16 muffin cups.
3. In a large bowl, mix the flour, cinnamon, baking soda, and salt.
4. In a separate bowl, mix the oil, eggs, and sugar.
5. Stir the oil mixture into the flour mixture just until moist. Fold in the peaches.
6. Spoon into the prepared muffin cups.
7. Bake 25 minutes in the preheated oven, until a toothpick inserted in the center of a muffin comes out clean.
8. Cool 10 minutes before turning out onto wire racks to cool completely.

Spiced Peach Oatmeal Muffins

Ingredients:

1 cup quick cooking oats
1 cup buttermilk
1/3 cup brown sugar
1/3 cup applesauce
1/4 cup molasses
2 eggs
1 1/3 cups all-purpose flour
1 tsp. baking soda
1 tsp. baking powder
1 1/2 cups pitted and diced fresh peaches
2 tbsps. white sugar
1/2 tsp. ground cinnamon

Directions:

1. Preheat oven to 400 degrees F (200 degrees C). Grease muffin cups or line with paper muffin liners.
2. In a large bowl, mix together oats, buttermilk, brown sugar, applesauce, molasses and eggs.
3. In a separate bowl, stir together flour, baking soda and baking powder. Stir flour mixture into eggs mixture, just until moistened.
4. Fold in peaches.
5. Spoon batter into prepared muffin cups.
6. Bake in preheated oven for 15 minutes.
7. While muffins are baking, combine 2 tbsps. sugar and 1/2 tsp. cinnamon.
8. After 15 minutes of baking, remove muffins from oven and sprinkle with cinnamon sugar.
9. Return to oven and continue baking for 3 minutes, until a toothpick inserted into center of a muffin comes out clean.

Peach, Basil & Cheddar Muffins

Ingredients:

4 fresh peaches, cut into 1/2-inch pieces
4 tsps. finely minced fresh basil
1 tbsp. brown sugar
1 1/2 cups all-purpose flour
1 1/2 tsps. baking powder
1/2 tsp. baking soda
1/2 tsp. salt
1 cup shredded extra-sharp Cheddar cheese
1/2 cup butter, room temperature
7 tbsps. brown sugar
2 eggs, room temperature
1/4 cup shredded extra-sharp Cheddar cheese

Directions:

1. Preheat oven to 350 degrees F (175 degrees C).
2. Grease 12 muffin cups or line with paper liners.
3. Mix peaches, basil, and 1 tbsp. brown sugar in a bowl.
4. Let sit until sugar dissolves, about 15 minutes.
5. Sift flour, baking powder, baking soda, and salt together in a large bowl.
6. Mix 1 cup Cheddar cheese into flour mixture.
7. Beat butter and 7 tbsps. brown sugar in a bowl with an electric mixer until smooth and creamy.
8. Add eggs, one at a time, until just combined; gently fold in peaches.
9. Mix flour mixture, a little at time, into peach mixture until batter is just combined.
10. Spoon batter into the prepared muffin cups. Sprinkle 1/4 cup Cheddar cheese over batter.
11. Bake in the preheated oven until a toothpick inserted in the middle of a muffin comes out clean, about 25 minutes.

Peach Sweet and Sour Sauce

Ingredients:

3 tbsps. chicken broth
2 tbsps. peach preserves
1 tbsp. sherry vinegar
1 pinch Chinese five-spice powder
1 pinch cayenne pepper
Salt and ground black pepper to taste

Directions:

1. Whisk chicken broth, peach preserves, sherry vinegar, Chinese five-spice powder, and cayenne pepper in a saucepan over medium-high heat.
2. Bring to a boil.
3. Cook until reduced and slightly thickened, 5 minutes.
4. Season with salt and black pepper to taste.

Tuna Fish Tacos

Ingredients:

1 (15.25 oz.) can lite peach slices, drained and chopped
1 (4.25 oz.) can chopped green chilies, drained
1/4 cup finely chopped red onion
1 tbsp. fresh chopped parsley
1 tbsp. fresh squeezed lime juice
1/4 tsp. hot pepper sauce

Tacos Ingredients:

1 (5 oz.) can albacore tuna packed in water, drained and flaked
8 (6 inch) corn, flour, or whole wheat tortillas, slightly warmed
Finely shredded green cabbage (optional)
Shredded Monterey Jack cheese (optional)
Lime wedges (optional)

Salsa Directions:

1. In medium bowl combine chopped peaches, green chiles, red onion, parsley, lime juice and Tabasco sauce.
2. Cover and refrigerate until ready to serve.

Taco Directions:

1. Fill tortillas with flaked tuna; top with peach salsa.
2. Serve with shredded cabbage and cheese if desired.
3. Garnish with lime wedges if desired.

Peach Sangria

Ingredients:

4 large fresh peaches - peeled, pitted, and sliced
1 cup hot water
1/2 cup light brown sugar
1 pinch ground cinnamon
2 1/2 cups dry white wine
1/2 cup triple sec liqueur
1 (750 milliliter) bottle sparkling white wine, chilled

Directions:

1. Blend peaches, hot water, brown sugar, and cinnamon in a blender or food processor until smooth.
2. Transfer to a pitcher; stir in dry white wine and triple sec.
3. Cover and chill in refrigerator for at least 4 hours.
4. Strain peach mixture through a large cheesecloth-lined sieve; squeeze cloth to remove all the juices.
5. Pour juice into a large pitcher; stir in sparkling white wine.

Honeyed Peach Pancake Syrup

Ingredients:

6 cups thickly sliced peaches with peels
3 cups water
1 cup honey, or more to taste
3 tbsps. freshly squeezed lemon juice, or to taste

Directions:

1. Combine peaches and water in a nonreactive 3-quart pot.
2. Bring to a boil. Reduce heat and simmer until peaches are soft and have colored the liquid, 20 to 25 minutes.
3. Strain peaches and their juice through a fine-mesh sieve set over a bowl.
4. Let peaches stand, occasionally giving them a gentle press with the back of a spoon, 5 minutes.
5. Discard peach solids.
6. Return strained juice to pot. Stir in honey to taste.
7. Bring to a boil. Skim off and discard any foam that appears on top.
8. Taste and add lemon juice to adjust sweetness.
9. Pour hot syrup into clean half-pint jars or bottles, leaving 1/2 inch headspace and using wide-mouth jars if freezing.
10. Wipe rims clean with a damp paper towel.
11. Let cool completely (about 1 hour). Apply clean lids.
12. Store in fridge up to 3 weeks or in freezer up to 6 months.

Mascarpone Stuffed French Toast with Peaches

8 fresh peaches
1/2 cup sugar
4 pinches ground nutmeg
1/2 tsp. ground cinnamon
4 Mexican bolillo rolls
1 cup mascarpone cheese
6 tbsps. confectioners' sugar
1 lemon, zested 6 eggs
3/4 cup milk
1/2 tsp. vanilla extract
2 tsps. butter, or as needed
2 tsps. vegetable oil, or as needed

Directions:

1. Peel peaches, remove pits, and slice into a heavy saucepan, catching all the juices.
2. Stir in sugar, nutmeg, and cinnamon, and cook over medium heat until bubbly.
3. Continue cooking, stirring occasionally, until the sauce reaches a syrupy consistency, about 10 minutes.
4. Remove from heat.
5. Meanwhile, cut off and discard the ends of the bolillo rolls.
6. Slice the rolls into 1 1/4-inch-thick slices.
7. Lay each slice of bread on a board, and with a sharp knife held parallel to the board, cut a pocket into each slice, leaving three sides intact. Set aside.
8. Stir together the mascarpone, confectioners' sugar, and lemon zest until smooth. Scoop this mixture into a small plastic bag.
9. Cut off one corner of the bag, and pipe as much filling into the pocket in each slice of bread as will fit without overflowing.
10. Whisk together the eggs, milk, and vanilla in a shallow bowl.
11. Melt butter with oil over medium heat in a large nonstick skillet.
12. Dip each stuffed piece of bread into the batter, add to the skillet, and cook until browned on both sides.
13. Serve hot with the warm peach sauce.

Champagne Peach Punch

Ingredients:

3 (11.5 oz.) cans peach nectar
1 (6 oz.) can frozen orange juice concentrate
1/4 cup lemon juice
1/2 cup peach brandy
1/4 cup grenadine syrup
1 (32 fluid oz.) bottle carbonated water
3 (750 milliliter) bottles champagne

Directions:

1. Chill all ingredients. In a large punch bowl combine peach nectar, concentrated orange juice, lemon juice, brandy and grenadine.
2. Mix well and pour in the carbonated water and champagne.

Peach Apple Salsa

Ingredients:

1 cup diced peaches
1/2 cup diced apple
1/2 cup diced avocado
1/2 cup diced tomato
1/3 cup chopped green onion
1/4 cup chopped fresh cilantro
2 tbsps. lemon juice
2 tbsps. olive oil
1 tsp. toasted sesame oil
1 tsp. ground cumin
1 jalapeno pepper, seeded and minced
Salt and ground black pepper to taste

Directions:

1. Mix peaches, apple, avocado, tomato, green onion, cilantro, lemon juice, olive oil, sesame oil, cumin, jalapeno pepper, salt, and black pepper together in a bowl.
2. Cover with plastic wrap and refrigerate for flavors to blend, at least 3 hours.

Peach Pear Salsa

Ingredients:

1 tbsp. olive oil
1/2 red onion, diced
2 cloves garlic, minced
4 peaches - pitted and diced
1 pear, peeled, cored, and diced
1/4 cup honey
1 tsp. curry powder
Salt and pepper to taste

Directions:

1. Heat the olive oil in a small skillet over medium-low heat; cook the onion and garlic in the hot oil until translucent, about 5 minutes.
2. Stir the peaches, pear, and honey into the onion and garlic mixture; allow to cook together for 2 minutes.
3. Season with the curry powder, salt, and pepper.
4. Continue cooking at a simmer until hot, 5 to 6 minutes.

Spicy Strawberry Kiwi Peach Salsa

Ingredients:

1 ripe peach, peeled, pitted, and diced
1 kiwi, peeled and diced
4 fresh strawberries, diced
1/2 jalapeno pepper, seeded and diced
1 tbsp. lime juice
1 green onion, chopped
2 tbsps. chopped fresh cilantro
1 pinch salt

Directions:

1. Combine the peach, kiwi, strawberries, jalapeno pepper, lime juice, green onion, cilantro, and salt in a bowl.
2. Gently stir to combine.

Peach and Strawberry Sorbet

Ingredients:

2 cups sliced fresh peaches
1 cup fresh strawberries, hulled
1 cup fresh orange juice
1/4 cup brown sugar

Directions:

1. Place the peaches, strawberries, orange juice, and brown sugar in a food processor.
2. Puree until smooth.
3. Pour mixture into an ice cream maker and freeze according to manufacturer's instructions until firm.

Peach and Lavender Ice

Ingredients:

2 pounds sliced frozen peaches, thawed
1 1/2 cups white sugar
1/2 cup dried lavender flowers
3 tbsps. lemon juice
3 cups water

Directions:

1. Freeze in a 6-quart ice cream maker according to manufacturer's instructions.

Georgia Peach Homemade Ice Cream

Ingredients:

2 1/2 pounds fresh peaches, peeled, pitted and chopped
1/2 cup white sugar
1 pint half-and-half cream
1 (14 oz.) can sweetened condensed milk
1 (12 fluid oz.) can evaporated milk
1 tsp. vanilla extract
2 cups whole milk, or as needed

Directions:

1. Puree peaches with the sugar and half-and-half in batches in a blender or food processor.
2. In a gallon ice cream freezer container, mix together the peach mixture, sweetened condensed milk, evaporated milk, and vanilla.
3. Pour in enough whole milk to fill the container to the fill line, about 2 cups.
4. Follow the manufacturer's instructions to freeze the ice cream.

Peach Pie with Sour Cream

Ingredients:

1 1/4 cups all-purpose flour
1/2 cup butter, cut into chunks
1/2 tsp. salt
2 tbsps. sour cream
4 fresh peaches, peeled, pitted, and sliced
3 egg yolks
2 tbsps. all-purpose flour
1/3 cup sour cream
1 cup white sugar

Directions:

1. Preheat oven to 425 degrees F (220 degrees C).
2. Butter a 9-inch pie dish.
3. Place 1 1/4 cups flour, butter, salt, and 2 tbsps. sour cream in a food processor; pulse until mixture comes together in a large ball.
4. Press dough into prepared pie dish to form a crust.
5. Bake in preheated hoven until golden brown, about 10 minutes.
6. Remove pie crust from oven.
7. Reduce oven heat to 350 degrees F (175 degrees C).
8. Arrange peach slices in pie crust.
9. Lightly beat egg yolks in a large bowl. Add in sugar, 1/3 cup sour cream, and 2 tbsps. flour; stir until well-mixed.
10. Pour egg mixture over peaches. Cover pie with aluminum foil.
11. Bake in preheated oven for 50 minutes; remove foil.
12. Continue baking until peach filling is set, about 15 minutes more.

Grilled Peaches and Cream

Ingredients:

4 peaches, halved and pitted
2 tbsps. clover honey
1 cup soft cream cheese with honey and nuts
1 tbsp. vegetable oil

Directions:

1. Preheat a grill for medium-high heat.
2. Brush peaches with a light coating of oil.
3. Place pit side down onto the grill.
4. Grill for 5 minutes, or until the surfaces have nice grill marks.
5. Turn the peaches over, and drizzle with a bit of honey.
6. Place a dollop of the cream cheese spread in the place where the pit was.
7. Grill for 2 to 3 more minutes, or until the filling is warm.
8. Serve immediately.

Peaches and Cream

Ingredients:

1 large fresh peach, peeled, pitted and sliced
1 tsp. brown sugar
2 tbsps. sour cream
1 tbsp. chopped pecans

Directions:

1. Place sliced peach in a small serving dish.
2. Sprinkle with brown sugar and spoon sour cream on top.
3. Sprinkle with pecans.

Grilled Peaches

Ingredients:

3 tbsps. white sugar
3/4 cup balsamic vinegar
2 tsps. freshly ground black peppercorns
2 large fresh peaches with peel, halved and pitted
2 1/2 oz. blue cheese, crumbled

Directions:

1. In a saucepan over medium heat, stir together the white sugar, balsamic vinegar, and pepper.
2. Simmer until liquid has reduced by one half. It should become slightly thicker. Remove from heat, and set aside.
3. Preheat grill for medium-high heat.
4. Lightly oil the grill grate. Place peaches on the prepared grill, cut side down.
5. Cook for about 5 minutes, or until the flesh is caramelized.
6. Turn peaches over. Brush the top sides with the balsamic glaze, and cook for another 2 to 3 minutes.
7. Transfer the peach halves to individual serving dishes, and drizzle with remaining glaze. Sprinkle with crumbled blue cheese.

Peach Brulee

Ingredients:

1 (15 oz.) can peach halves, drained
1/4 cup packed brown sugar
1/4 tsp. ground cinnamon
1/4 cup coarsely chopped pecans

Directions:

1. Arrange peach halves, cut-side up in a shallow baking dish.
2. In a small dish, stir together the brown sugar, cinnamon, and chopped pecans.
3. Sprinkle the mixture over the peaches.
4. Broil 3 inches from heat for 2 to 3 minutes, or until the topping is browned.
5. Serve with whipped cream or vanilla ice cream.

Peach Bread Pudding with Caramel Sauce

Ingredients:

2 cups fresh peaches - peeled, pitted and halved
1 (14 oz.) can sweetened condensed milk
3 eggs, lightly beaten
1 1/4 cups hot water
1/4 cup butter, melted
1 tsp. ground cinnamon
1 tsp. vanilla extract 4 cups French bread, torn into small pieces

Caramel Sauce Ingredients:

1/2 cup brown sugar
1/2 cup butter
2 tbsps. light corn syrup
1 tbsp. rum

Directions:

1. Preheat an oven to 325 degrees F (165 degrees C).
2. Grease a 9x13-inch baking dish.
3. Chop the peaches and lightly mash them in a mixing bowl.
4. Combine the sweetened condensed milk and the eggs; add them to the peaches and mix well.
5. Stir in the hot water, melted butter, cinnamon, and vanilla.
6. Stir the French bread into to the custard mixture until the bread is completely moistened.
7. Turn the pudding into the prepared baking dish.
8. Bake until a knife inserted in the center of the pudding comes out clean, about 1 hour and 10 minutes.
9. While the pudding is baking, combine the brown sugar, 1/2 cup butter, corn syrup, and rum in a saucepan.
10. Bring to a boil over medium heat and simmer for 3 to 4 minutes or until just slightly thickened.
11. Let cool slightly.
12. Remove the pudding from the oven and let it cool for about ten minutes before serving. Serve warm with the caramel sauce.
13. Cool and cover any leftover pudding and store it in the refrigerator.

Peaches and Cream Pie

Ingredients:

3/4 cup all-purpose flour
1/2 tsp. salt
1 tsp. baking powder
1 (3 oz.) package non-instant vanilla pudding mix
3 tbsps. butter, softened
1 egg
1/2 cup milk
1 (29 oz.) can sliced peaches, drained and syrup reserved
1 (8 oz.) package cream cheese, softened
1/2 cup white sugar
1 tbsp. white sugar
1 tsp. ground cinnamon

Directions:

1. Preheat oven to 350 degrees F (175 degrees C).
2. Grease sides and bottom of a 10 inch deep-dish pie pan.
3. In a medium mixing bowl, mix together flour, salt, baking powder and pudding mix.
4. Mix in butter, egg and milk. Beat for 2 minutes.
5. Pour mixture into pie pan. Arrange the peach slices on top of the pudding mixture.
6. In a small mixing bowl, beat cream cheese until fluffy.
7. Add 1/2 cup sugar and 3 tbsps. reserved peach syrup.
8. Beat for 2 minutes.
9. Spoon mixture over peaches to within 1 inch of pan edge.
10. Mix together 1 tbsp. sugar and 1 tsp. cinnamon, and sprinkle over top.
11. Bake in preheated oven for 30 to 35 minutes, until golden brown.
12. Chill before serving.

Peach and Escarole Salad

Ingredients:

2 tbsps. olive oil
1 tbsp. rice vinegar
1 tbsp. sherry vinegar
1 tsp. mayonnaise
Salt and ground black pepper to taste
1 small head escarole, cut into 1-inch ribbons
1 peach, sliced
4 oz. goat cheese, crumbled
1/2 cup toasted walnuts

Directions:

1. Whisk olive oil, rice vinegar, sherry vinegar, mayonnaise, salt, and black pepper in a bowl until smooth.
2. Place escarole, peach slices, goat cheese, and walnuts in a large bowl.
3. Drizzle in vinegar mixture and toss to coat.

Peach and Berry Salad

Ingredients:

3 fresh peaches
2 1/2 pints blackberries
1 pint strawberries, hulled and sliced
1/4 cup honey
1/2 tsp. ground cardamom

Directions:

1. Bring medium pot of water to boil.
2. Add peaches and blanch for 30 seconds.
3. Drain and transfer to medium bowl.
4. Cover with cold water and cool. Drain, peel and slice.
5. In a medium bowl, combine peaches, blackberries, strawberries, honey and cardamom. Toss together and refrigerate.

Peach Salad with Raspberry Vinaigrette

Ingredients:

1 (10 oz.) package fresh spinach
1/2 cup chopped almonds
1/3 cup sliced red onion
1/4 cup grated Asiago cheese
1/2 cup raspberry vinaigrette dressing
Salt and ground black pepper to taste
2 fresh peaches, sliced

Directions:

1. Combine spinach, almonds, onion, and Asiago cheese in a large bowl.
2. Drizzle dressing over salad and season with salt and pepper.
3. Add peaches and toss.

Minty Peach Chicken Salad

Ingredients:

3 fresh peaches, peeled, pitted, and cubed
2 cups cubed cooked chicken breast
1 cucumber, seeded and chopped

Dressing Ingredients:

1/4 cup white wine vinegar
1/4 cup minced fresh mint
1/3 cup white sugar
1 tbsp. lemon juice
1/4 tsp. salt
1/8 tsp. ground black pepper
3 dashes hot sauce, or to taste
2 avocados - peeled, pitted, and cubed

Directions:

1. Combine peaches, chicken, and cucumber in a large bowl.
2. Blend vinegar, mint, sugar, lemon juice, salt, pepper, and hot sauce in a blender until vinaigrette is smooth.
3. Drizzle vinaigrette over peach mixture; toss to coat.
4. Cover bowl with plastic wrap and refrigerate until chilled, at least 30 minutes.
5. Fold avocado into salad before serving.

Peach and Tomato Caprese Salad

Ingredients:

2 tbsps. extra-virgin olive oil
1 tbsp. balsamic vinegar
1 tsp. flaked salt, divided
2 large heirloom tomatoes, thinly sliced
2 ripe peaches - halved, pitted, and sliced into half moons
6 leaves fresh basil
1 (8 oz.) ball fresh mozzarella, thinly sliced

Directions:

1. Whisk olive oil, balsamic vinegar, and 1 pinch flaked salt together in a bowl until dressing is smooth.
2. Alternate tomato slices, peach slices, basil leaves, and mozzarella slices in layers on a platter.
3. Drizzle dressing over salad and sprinkle remaining flaked salt on top.

Peach Bow Tie Salad

Ingredients:

1 cup farfalle (bow tie) pasta
10 oz. spinach
1 head romaine lettuce, roughly torn
2 peaches, peeled, pitted, and diced, or more to taste
3/4 cup poppy seed dressing
2 cups diced cooked chicken (optional)

Directions:

1. Bring a large pot of lightly salted water to a boil.
2. Cook the bow-tie pasta at a boil, stirring occasionally, until cooked through yet firm to the bite, about 12 minutes.
3. Drain and run under cold water to cool.
4. Combine pasta, spinach, romaine lettuce, and peaches in a large bowl.
5. Add poppy seed dressing and toss to coat.
6. Top salad with chicken.

Peach Smoothie

Ingredients:

1 large peach, sliced and frozen
1 banana, cut into pieces and frozen
1/2 cup orange juice
1/2 cup soy milk
1 tbsp. ground flax seed (optional)

Directions:

1. Blend peach, banana, orange juice, soy milk, and flax seed in a blender until smooth.

Peach Banana Smoothie

Ingredients:

1 cup plain yogurt
1 (15.25 oz.) can peaches
2 bananas, sliced
1/4 cup orange juice
1/4 cup white sugar, or to taste
2 cubes ice

Directions:

1. Blend yogurt, peaches, bananas, orange juice, sugar, and ice in a blender on high until the ice is crushed and the smoothie is to your desired consistency.

Peach Pudding

Ingredients:

1/4 cup peach or apricot gelatin
1/2 cup hot milk
1-1/2 cups cold milk
1 pkg. (3.4 oz.) instant vanilla pudding mix
Sliced fresh peaches and whipped topping, optional

Directions:

1. In a large bowl, dissolve gelatin powder in hot milk; set aside.
2. Meanwhile, in a large bowl, beat cold milk and dry pudding mix on low speed for 2 minutes. beat in gelatin mixture.
3. Let stand for 5 minutes. Spoon into individual dishes.
4. Garnish with peaches and whipped topping if desired.

About the Author

Laura Sommers is **The Recipe Lady!**

She is the #1 Best Selling Author of over 80 recipe books.

She is a loving wife and mother who lives on a small farm in Baltimore County, Maryland and has a passion for all things domestic especially when it comes to saving money. She has a profitable eBay business and is a couponing addict. Follow her tips and tricks to learn how to make delicious meals on a budget, save money or to learn the latest life hack!

Visit her Amazon Author Page to see her latest books:

amazon.com/author/laurasommers

Visit the Recipe Lady's blog for even more great recipes and to learn which books are **FREE** for download each week:

http://the-recipe-lady.blogspot.com/

Subscribe to The Recipe Lady blog through Amazon and have recipes and updates sent directly to your Kindle:

The Recipe Lady Blog through Amazon

Laura Sommers is also an Extreme Couponer and Penny Hauler! If you would like to find out how to get things for **FREE** with coupons or how to get things for only a **PENNY**, then visit her couponing blog **Penny Items and Freebies**

http://penny-items-and-freebies.blogspot.com/

Other books by Laura Sommers

- **Blackberry Recipes**
- **Strawberry Recipes**
- **Blueberry Recipes**

May all of your meals be a banquet
with good friends and good food.

Made in the USA
Las Vegas, NV
17 August 2023

76242295R00037